A COMMENTARY SERIES ON JOHN'S GOSPEL

THAT YE SHOULD KNOW

Volume One: Chapters 1-4

PASTOR E. HERSCHBERG
PASTOR GEORGE W. ADAIR

Betrothed
Messianic Imprint
of Little Roni Publishers LLC

Betrothed
Messianic Imprint of Little Roni Publishers
Clanton, Alabama
www.littleronipublishers.com
ISBN-13: 979-8-9890806-4-9
Also available in eBook
V11162023SC

Cover Image: Jerusalem Wall © Denis Doukhan, Pixabay.com, licensed.

PUBLISHED IN THE UNITED STATES OF AMERICA

Dedications

Pastor E. Herschberg

First and foremost, I dedicate this work to the Lord God of the Holy Bible, and to my beloved wife, Cindy. Next, I dedicate this to our ministry, Sound the Shofar Messianic Ministries, and to my family, and all my dear friends at my workplace. May God's blessings be with all of you.

Pastor George W. Adair

I would like to dedicate this in loving memory of Doragail Adair. We would like to thank Ellen Sallas for all the work to make this book possible.

Both pastors would also like to thank Candy Coffee for technical support.

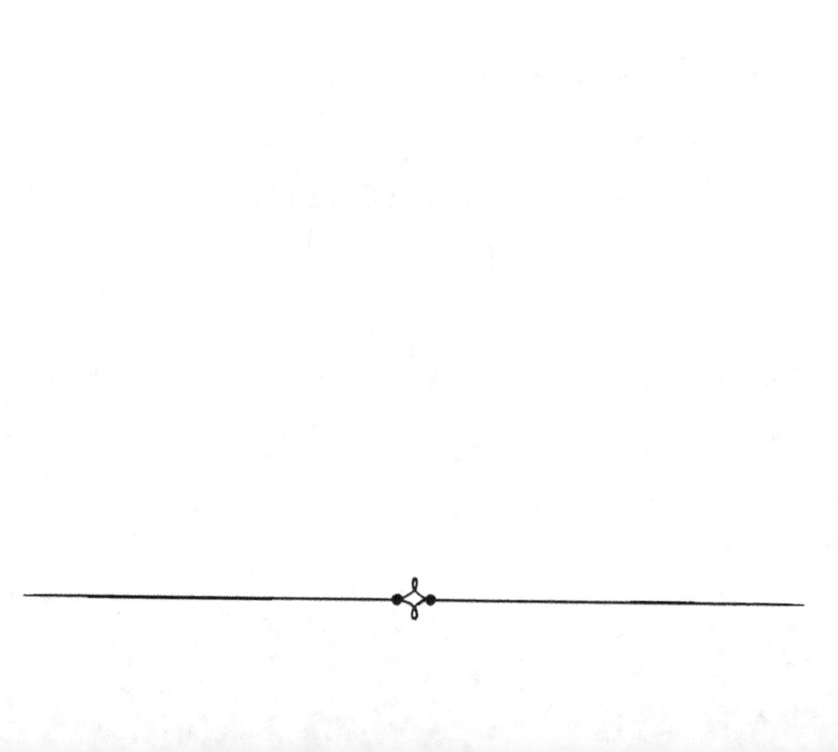

Table of Contents

Introduction

THE GOSPEL OF JOHN IS THE PERSONAL, EYEWITNESS testimony of the words and works of the Messiah of Israel from the perspective of a simple first century Israeli fisherman, called by God.

John's gospel is a theologically detailed work with an emphasis on the deity and divinity of Messiah Yeshua[1] that some would say, is preached and taught as the "God loves the world" Gospel and limited to that aspect alone. From a Jewish perspective, it is at times looked at as the antisemitic Gospel because of the use of the term "the Jews," and sadly, on occasion, this sentiment is unknowingly (we hope)

---

[1] Yeshua is Jesus' name in Hebrew; it means literally, "Salvation."

conveyed from church pulpits. Then there is the liberal Christian and secular academics' perspective that questions the claims and legitimacy of John's Gospel due to the late dating of his writing, even trying to further date it past John's lifetime.

IS JOHN'S GOSPEL
ABOUT MORE THAN
"GOD'S LOVE"?

Our question today is, why? Why limit John's Gospel to "God's love" only? Why portray it in an antisemitic light? Why attempt to discredit John's Gospel as a much later writing, thereby making it not even his?

The reasons are many, from the development of replacement theology and antisemitism of some of the early church fathers, to the liberalizing of the faith in more modern times. Whatever the reasons may be, it is because of the aforementioned, and most importantly, the Lord's calling, that we felt compelled to write this commentary. We believe John and his Gospel should be presented in its correct historical, theological, geographical, and cultural context, at least as close as possible. Why? Because it is God's holy Word, and it should be handled with the utmost reverence and care. This means presenting John's Gospel in the way the apostle wrote and intended it, as well as presenting the apostle as he was.

We are writing this book with the intention of removing the false assumption of John's Gospel being antisemitic by presenting both John and his Gospel in their original historical Jewish context in which he wrote.

Lastly, we are writing this because we want all people to understand that John's ultimate intention in his Gospel is that people will realize that Jesus is not only the Messiah of Israel, the only begotten Son of God, God in the form of flesh, but also the only way of salvation. As the title of this book and series is called, "That Ye Should Know".

Historical Background Information

WHO WAS JOHN, AND WHEN DID HE RECORD HIS GOSPEL? In some early church traditions, the Gospel writer is known as "Saint John the Theologian," and "Saint John the Evangelist." But what does the Bible (and history, for that matter) say concerning who and what John is?

The name "John" is the English, translated name; the writer's actual name is Hebrew, "Yochanan."[2] Yochanan was a fisherman by trade, in first century Israel, from the Galilean region (Matthew4:21-22). Yochanan lived from 6 A.D. to around 100 A.D. His last writing was the book of

---

[2] Yochanan is a Hebrew male name that means, "God is gracious."

Revelation, which he recorded around 96 A.D., while a prisoner on the island of Patmos (Revelation 1:9).

The apostle was Jewish, as is evident in his writings, reflecting obedience to Torah observance out of love, as Messiah Yeshua commanded (John 14:15, 1 John 5:1-3, Revelation 14:12). Another thing that the apostle's writings reveal about him is that he was both a brilliant theologian and eschatologist, which can be seen in the opening of his Gospel as well as in various parts of his other writings. One key thing that the Gospels reveal concerning Yochanan's character is that he was humble with an extremely caring nature toward fellow believers. This is evident in the wording he uses in his first epistle when addressing believers, stating, "My little children," and "Brethren" (1 John 2:1, 7).

According to the Gospel accounts, Yochanan's relationship with Yeshua the Messiah was very close. All the key events mentioned in the Gospels show that he was present and a part of Messiah's inner circle (Matthew 17:1-13, 26:37), and is very clearly seen at the last Passover Seder (John 13:23). Excluding legends and traditions, we can conclude that the Gospels reveal that Yochanan was from a hardworking background, had a very humble nature, was learned and mature in his Jewish identity, and was well versed in the Tanach, otherwise known as the "Old Testament" Scriptures.

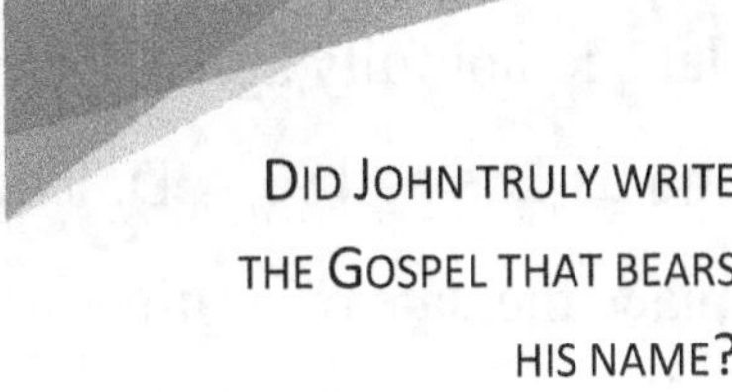

DID JOHN TRULY WRITE
THE GOSPEL THAT BEARS
HIS NAME?

This brings us to the question, when and where did Yochanan (John) write his Gospel? Also, did John actually write the Gospel that bears his name?

Although the Gospel itself does not indicate a clear autograph, it does clearly identify its author (John 21:20-24). The one who Yeshua loved is the one who, "testifieth of these things and wrote these things" (v:24).

Does this Gospel meet the qualifications of being part of the canon of Scripture (2nd Timothy 3:16)? "And we know that his testimony is true" (v:24). Yes, it is true that unlike the opening of Revelation, where John makes it clear outright, that it is he by name, the closing of this Gospel makes perfectly obvious the one who penned it.

Now let us take a look at the time and place in which it was written.

The dates and location John's Gospel was written in is somewhat sketchy as a variety of commentaries and scholars do not fully agree. Dates range from as early as 70 A.D. to as late as 180 A.D. There are even some scholars that place the date of writing prior to 70 A.D.

After personal research, this is what we have concluded. We do not believe the Gospel could have been written during or prior to 70 A.D, and here is why. The temple in Jerusalem was destroyed in 70 A.D. under the Roman emperor, Titus. The three synoptic Gospels, Matthew, Mark, and Luke, all contain the famous eschatological sermon on the Mount of Olives which Yeshua delivered after He chased the merchants out of the temple. The sermon begins with the disciples marveling over the magnificent architecture of the temple. Yeshua goes on to prophesy the temple's destruction, which occurred in 70 A.D. This is the key reason the first three Gospels can be dated prior to 70 A.D. and John's would not be. John's Gospel does not contain this sermon most likely because the event had already happened. Likewise, a date past 100 A.D. would not be possible because John would no longer have been alive to record it.

We believe the apostle recorded his Gospel sometime between the later 70's and mid 80's A.D. given that the book of Revelation was his last recorded work. We also believe that based on the fact that the Gospel that bears his name, that it is John's writing, meets the qualifications to be part of the canon of Scripture.

John Chapter 1: Theology of God and Messiah

"IN THE BEGINNING WAS THE WORD, AND THE Word was with God, and the Word was God. The same was in the beginning with God. All things were made by Him; and without Him was not any thing made that was made. In Him was life; and the life was the light of men. And the light shineth in darkness; and the darkness comprehended it not."

John 1: 1-5

Verses 1 - 5

The Koine Greek here is "En arka" (in the beginning). The apostle begins his Gospel by repeating the words of Moses in Genesis One. In fact, John uses the Greek equivalent of the Hebrew for, "In the beginning," *Beret-sheet*. Looking at the context of these first five verses, it becomes clear that the apostle did this intentionally. Why? Because John is confirming the biblical creation account, that all things were created by God, and nothing came into existence without God. However, John not only reiterates this truth of Moses, but goes on to elaborate on God's identity, showing the tri-unity of the God of Creation.

JOHN OPENS HIS GOSPEL PRECISELY AS MOSES OPENED THE BIBLE IN GENESIS 1:1.

In Genesis 1:1, the Hebrew word used for God is "Elohim." Not the title of God (Adonai), not the descriptive term of God Almighty (El-Shaddai), nor the personal name of God (the four Hebrew letters known as the tetragrammaton), but rather the general term for God, "Elohim," which translates as "mighty one" and connotates judgment. In keeping with our current topic, the word "Elohim" is a plural word for God, yet there is only one

God (Exodus 20:1-3, Deuteronomy 6:4). Here in John 1, the word used for God is the Greek general term (Theos) which is the equivalent to the Hebrew (Elohim). So, why would Moses use a plural form for the only one true God? The answer is found here, in John 1:1.

Elohim is the Father and Yeshua, this is the plural form of God in Genesis 1. Yeshua in John 1 is 'Theos' which is 'Elohim' in Genesis 1:1, Father and Son. In (vv:2-5) is confirmation of Yeshua in verse 1 as it describes that the creation process did not happen without His presence and involvement, from the light of the world (Gen 1:3), to the creation of man, and life entering into Him (Gen 1:26-29, 2:7). All of creation happened by the Father, Yeshua, and the Ruach ha' Kodesh[3] (Gen 1:1-2). John clearly demonstrates through the creation account that Messiah Yeshua is God in the form of flesh, the second Person of the tri-unity of the one and only God of Israel.

Yeshua's involvement in the creation process is solidified in verses 2-3: "All things were made by him." The Gospel writer wants to make this fact known to his

---

[3] Ruach ha' kodesh – Hebrew, literally "breath of God," the Holy Spirit.

readers. Creation would not and could not have occurred without Him, again, because He is the second Person of the one true God of creation. Next, in verse 4, John shows how Messiah Yeshua is the life of humanity and the light of the world; this is consistent with the work of God during the creation process (Genesis 1:3-4, 26, 2:7). We also see the imagery of the light of Messiah Yeshua elsewhere in John's writings in the book of Revelation where He is represented as the "Shammesh,"[4] of the Menorah, the light source that gives light to the other congregations of believers (Revelation 1:12-13).

> There was a man sent from God, whose name was John. The same came for a witness, to bear witness of the Light, that all men through him might believe. He was not that Light, but was sent to bear witness of that Light. That was the true Light, which lighteth every man that cometh into the world. He was in the world, and the world was made by him, and the world knew him not.
>
> John 1: 6-10

---

[4] Hebrew for "servant," the middle candle of the menorah.

Verses 6 - 10

In verse 6, the writer begins a new account concerning the Messiah Yeshua, His announcer. Verse 6 speaks of a certain man that was sent by God whose name is also John.

Who is this John? It first must be made clear that this is not this Gospel's writer, the apostle John (Yochanan). The John that is being spoken of here is related to Yeshua through His mother Mariam (the Hebrew name of Mary) Elizabeth, the cousin of Mary, the mother of Messiah Yeshua. The full account of this is in Luke's Gospel (Luke 1:58-80). This is the one known in all the Gospels as "John the baptizer." So, the question is, who is this John and what is his role concerning Messiah Yeshua?

John the baptizer was the son of a priest of the temple, which means this John was a Levite. Verse 6 of John's Gospel says he (John the baptizer) was "sent by God." What does this mean? John the baptizer is the fulfillment of two specific prophecies in the Tanakh (Old Testament).

First, he is the one that announces the Messiah's coming and prepares the people to receive him (Isaiah 40:3-

5). Next, John the baptizer is also a partial fulfillment of Elijah from Malachi's prophecy (Malachi 3:1-5, 4:5). Will Elijah (himself) be in the last days? Yes, but that is a whole other discussion and book.

JOHN THE BAPTIZER'S
APPEARANCE FULFILLS
BIBLE PROPHECY
CONCERNING MESSIAH.

In verse 7, John is the witness of the Light; he saw and testified of who the Messiah is. The term "Light" here is in reference to the term used in the previous verses for the Messiah. The verse goes on to confirm that salvation only comes through belief in Him (Messiah) (Eph 2:8, John 14:6).

In verses 8-9, the following of John the baptizer becomes evident. The distinction between him and the Messiah is made clear. The messenger is only the witness, not the Messiah (Light) Himself. Only Messiah Yeshua is the true Light.

Verse 10 is the evidence from the result of the fall in

Genesis 3. How? The Creator is present among His creation and yet, the creation does not know Him. This is elaborated on in more detail in the next verse.

> He came unto His own, and His own received Him not. But as many as received Him, to them gave He power to become the sons of God, even to them that believe on His name: Which were born, not of blood, nor of the will of the flesh, nor of the will of man, but of God.
>
> And the Word was made flesh, and dwelt among us, (and we beheld his glory, the glory as of the only begotten of the Father,) full of grace and truth.
>
> John 1: 11-14

Verses 11 - 14

In verse 11, the beginning of two prophecies from the Tanakh concerning the Messiah is introduced. The Messiah would not be received and accepted by His own. This is foretold in the book of Psalms and in Isaiah, but the timing of this would not come to complete fruition until Yeshua's arrest, trial, and crucifixion (Psalm 22:7-8, Isaiah 53:3).

It is also important to understand that while it does refer

to His fellow Jewish people, it is actually referring to a specific group within His community, not the Jewish people as a whole. This will become evident as the Gospel account proceeds.

Verse 12 is a brief explanation of the privilege salvation comes with, becoming "sons of God', children of the Most High, through belief and faith in the Messiah Yeshua.

In verse 13, it speaks of being born, but not by the means of normal human birth. This is a spiritual rebirth that does not happen by human efforts or human will. This birth is by the will of God alone. God's gift of salvation through Yeshua, to those whom He ordained to receive Messiah and believe on Him. It is important to remember that God knew each and every human being before any of us ever came into this world (Jeremiah 1:5).

In verse 14, the Gospel writer again confirms that it is Yeshua who is the Word, the Word that is God (v:1), that now came in the form of flesh. The Koine Greek word for "flesh" here is, "sarx," which confirms that the Word is human. The Greek word for "tabernacle" is "skene". Skene, though, does not mean "dwelt," rather it is the equivalent to the Hebrew word, "sukkot," which means "tabernacle."

Throughout Scripture, "tabernacle" refers to the time of the Exodus, when the Israelites wandered through the Sinai region and dwelt in mobile structures, tents. This action, tabernacling with God, is commanded to be commemorated every year during the fall Feasts of the Lord (Leviticus 23:33-44). The wording John used here seems deliberate; he may be referring to the time Messiah came into the world. Something to think about.

> John bare witness of Him, and cried, saying, This was He of whom I spake, He that cometh after me is preferred before me: for He was before me. And of His fulness have all we received, and grace for grace. For the law was given by Moses, but grace and truth came by Jesus Christ. No man hath seen God at any time, the only begotten Son, which is in the bosom of the Father, He hath declared him.
>
> John 1:15-18

Verses 15 - 18

In verse 15, John gives his testimony concerning Messiah Yeshua. In his testimony he begins with Yeshua's preincarnate existence, "This was He of whom I spake, He that cometh after me is preferred before me". How can one know that this is what the baptizer is speaking of?

According to Luke's testimony, John the baptizer was born six months before Yeshua (Luke 1:57-66). How could Yeshua be *before* his first cousin, John the baptizer? The answer goes back to the first fourteen verses of this Gospel in John, the Gospel writer's, theology. This statement is also confirmed in Yeshua's own testimony concerning His eternality (Revelation 1:8,11, 22:13).

In verses 16-17, the baptizer continues his testimony that with Messiah's arrival comes "grace and truth". Does this mean that God did not show and offer grace and truth prior to this point in history? Not at all. We see countless examples throughout the Tanakh of God's grace. From the pleading of Abraham for the sparing of the cities of Sodom and Gomorrah (Genesis 18:22-33), to the rescuing of Israel from Egypt and bringing them into the Promised Land (Exodus 3:8-9), as well as many other examples in Scripture. God's truth is in every word from Genesis to Malachi, which is made clear in the New Testament (2Timothy 3:15-16) because it is God's own breathed words. This grace and truth has now come in fullness with Messiah's first arrival.

In verse 18, it says, "For the law was given by Moses." This must be read in the proper context, because often times it has been preached that the law (commandments) were literally "thought up" and then given to the children of Israel by Moses, as if they came from Moses himself. This is not the case! A careful exegetical read of Exodus 20 clearly proves this. From the opening of the chapter, it is clear that the commandments are not from Moses, but from God Himself. *"And God spake all these words, saying…"* (Exodus 20:1).

The commandments were from God and even written with His own finger (Deuteronomy 9:10). Biblically, the only part that Moses had with God's commandments is that God delivered them to Moses and then used Moses to deliver them to the children of Israel. The same God who gave His only begotten Son is the same God who wrote the commandments at Mount Sinai. He is the one true God; the same God from the "beginning" (John 1:1-2).

And this is the record of John, when the Jews sent priests and Levites from Jerusalem to ask him, Who art thou? And he confessed, and denied not; but confessed, I am not the Christ.

And they asked him, What then? Art thou Elias? And he saith, I am not. Art thou that prophet?

And he answered, No. Then said they unto him, Who art thou? that we may give an answer to them that sent us. What sayest thou of thyself?

He said, I am the voice of one crying in the wilderness, Make straight the way of the Lord, as said the prophet Esaias. And they which were sent were of the Pharisees.

John 1: 19-24

Verses 19 - 24

Verse nineteen makes it clear that this is the official record of John the baptizer. It is not a tale of folklore or ancient theory, but an official eyewitness firsthand account, which makes his testimony a documented historical record.

So, what is the baptizer's testimony?

The Jewish leadership (the sect of the Pharisees) sent

servants from the temple and members of the Levite tribe to question the baptizer. Why would the religious authority venture all the way out to the area of the Jordan river? Let us examine those reasons. One, at this point in first century Israel, it was the highly anticipated and expected time of the Messiah's arrival, as both history and prophetic passages of the Tanakh confirmed. And two, at this point in history, John the baptizer had a substantial following of Jewish people that were in eager expectation of the soon arrival of the Messiah (see John 3:30-35).

AT THIS POINT IN JEWISH HISTORY, MANY WERE EAGERLY EXPECTING MESSIAH'S ARRIVAL.

Because of the Messianic expectation and the following of the baptizer, the religious leaders verbalized their suspicions, alluding to the baptizer being the Messiah, or if John thought he was the Messiah. This is likely based on Israel's history at this time where a handful of individuals rose up on occasion to either start a separatist movement or a instigate a rebellion against the Roman occupation (see Rabbi Gamaliel's statement in the book of Acts, chapter 5:34-40).

Starting in verse twenty, a picture of the baptizer's humble and modest nature becomes evident when he immediately confesses that he is not the Messiah. The interrogation continues with the next question pertaining to an End Times prophecy pointed out earlier, "Art thou Elijah?" (V:21). Ask yourself, why would they ask the baptizer if he was Elijah? This is a good question, given that the prophet Elijah had been taken out of the world by God in the second book of Kings: *As they were walking along and talking together, suddenly a chariot of fire and horses of fire appeared and separated the two of them, and Elijah went up to heaven in a whirlwind."* (2 Kings 2:11 NIV).

The religious leaders asked this question in anticipation of Messiah's arrival, as they believed Elijah would come at the same time to fulfill Malachi's prophecy, *"See, I will send the prophet Elijah to you before that great and dreadful day of the Lord comes."* (Malachi 4:5 NIV)

John did, however, have a certain fulfillment in the

prophecy of Elijah's return, according to Yeshua, in that John was the announcer of Yeshua's arrival. *"And if you are willing to accept it, he [John the baptizer] is the Elijah who was to come."* (Matthew 11:14 NIV)

It is also noteworthy that later in Yeshua's ministry, the prophet Elijah appeared with Yeshua on Mount Tabor at the transfiguration and again proclaimed John the baptizer as Elijah (Matthew 17:1-13).

The next question is if John the baptizer was "that prophet"? What prophet were they referring to?

This would be the prophecy concerning a prophet being raised up among the Israelites that they would listen to. *"The Lord your God will raise up for you a prophet like Me from among you, from your fellow Israelites. You must listen to Him."* (Deuteronomy 18:15 NIV).

John's response again is "no," given that this prophecy is not concerning him, but in fact is referring to Messiah Yeshua and finds its fulfillment in Acts with the apostle Peter's sermon: *"For Moses truly said unto the fathers, 'a prophet shall the Lord your God raise up unto you of your brethren, like unto Me; Him shall ye hear in all things whatsoever He shall say unto you. And it shall come to pass, that every soul, which will not hear that prophet, shall be destroyed from among the people.'"* (Acts 3:22-23).

The Pharisees representatives finally ask John directly who he claims himself to be. John's response is a specific quote from the book of Isaiah, *"a voice crying out in the wilderness"* (Isaiah 40:3). John the baptizer is the one who would prepare the people for the Messiah's arrival. *This was John's divine calling and purpose.*

And they asked him, and said unto him, Why baptizest thou then, if thou be not that Christ, nor Elias, neither that prophet?

John answered them, saying, I baptize with water: but there standeth one among you, whom ye know not; He it is, who coming after me is preferred before me, whose shoe's latchet I am not worthy to unloose.

These things were done in Bethabara beyond Jordan, where John was baptizing. The next day John seeth Jesus coming unto him, and saith, Behold the Lamb of God, which taketh away the sin of the world.

John 1: 25-29

Verses 25 - 29

In verses 25 through 27, these representatives now ask John why he is baptizing people in water for the remission of sins if he is neither the Messiah, Elijah, nor "that prophet"? This act after all was performed by the tabernacle and temple priests before beginning their service to God. John's answer is threefold.

First, he tells them that one is coming that they do not know, either personally nor from the community. Next, the baptizer confirms the deity and divinity of the one who is coming by his statement, "He it is, who coming after me is preferred before me," (v:27). Again, Scripture makes it clear that John the baptizer came into the world six months before Yeshua, and John is out there, in the Jordan, baptizing and preaching before Yeshua was to arrive. So why would the baptizer claim that the one who is coming (Yeshua) is before him? Because Yeshua *was before him*, before John was ever born, before the world or anything came into existence (Genesis 1, John 1:1-14).

Lastly, we again witness the humility and humble

nature of John in the final part of his response, "whose shoe's latchet I am not worthy to unloose."

In verse 28, we are given specific geographical information of where in the Jordan this event occurred. In Bethabara. This region is east of Jerusalem, above the Dead Sea.

In verse 29, it is the day after the representatives from the temple interrogated the baptizer, and John sees Yeshua approaching. Notice the title he gives Yeshua, "the Lamb of God." Why would the baptizer use this particular phrasing in regard to the Messiah? John is using Passover imagery from (Exodus 12:1-36). The applied blood of a lamb without spot (no defects) saved the children of Israel when death came for the first born in Egypt. This was a prophetic picture of Yeshua's mock trial and sentencing to death by crucifixion, which took away the sins of the world, saving those who believe (Matthew 26:26-28). Notice the prophetic importance that it was Yeshua at the Last Passover (also called the Last Supper); his rushed trial and crucifixion occurs on the same day Israel was killing lambs at the temple to atone for their sins!

Messiah as a Lamb imagery is used again by John the

apostle in his description of the One in heaven who was worthy to open the scrolls and was the ruler from the Israelite tribe of Judah (Revelation 5:5). Why a lamb? Because it was a lamb that was offered as a sacrifice in the Old Testament as a sin offering (Leviticus 14:13). Yeshua, who is the Lamb of God, was a sacrifice for sin, the *final* sacrifice for sin for all time.

> This is he of whom I said, After me cometh a Man which is preferred before me: for He was before me. And I knew Him not: but that He should be made manifest to Israel, therefore am I come baptizing with water.
>
> And John bare record, saying, I saw the Spirit descending from heaven like a dove, and it abode upon Him. And I knew Him not: but He that sent me to baptize with water, the same said unto me, Upon whom thou shalt see the Spirit descending, and remaining on Him, the same is He which baptizeth with the Holy Ghost. And I saw, and bare record that this is the Son of God.
>
> John 1: 30-34

Verses 30 - 34

Here, John gives the account of what immediately followed when Yeshua emerged from the water, namely, the descending of the Ruach ha' Kodesh (Holy Spirit). John's Gospel does not cover the baptism of Yeshua like the other Gospels do, but it is clearly understood that it happened.

Next, John makes it clear about his spiritual limitations, that all he can possibly do is baptize with water. The One who is to come will baptize with so much more than water; He will baptize with the Holy Spirit (Matthew 3:11).

In verse 32, once again, the event is confirmed as a historically documented, eyewitness account. These verses close with a very important proclamation from the baptizer: "This is the Son of God." Previously, the baptizer called Him (Yeshua) the "Lamb of God," but now John calls Him "the Son of God." This proclamation, however, is coming from another Source other than John, the greatest Source of all – God the Father. The baptizer is only reiterating what God Himself proclaimed Yeshua to be, *"Thou art My beloved Son, in whom I am well pleased."* (Mark 1:11)

Again the next day after John stood, and two of his disciples; And looking upon Jesus as He walked, he saith, Behold the Lamb of God! And the two disciples heard him speak, and they followed Jesus.

Then Jesus turned, and saw them following, and saith unto them, What seek ye?

They said unto Him, Rabbi, (which is to say, being interpreted, Master,) where dwellest thou?

He saith unto them, Come and see.

They came and saw where He dwelt, and abode with Him that day: for it was about the tenth hour. One of the two which heard John speak, and followed Him, was Andrew, Simon Peter's brother. He first findeth his own brother Simon, and saith unto him, We have found the Messias, which is, being interpreted, the Christ.

John 1: 35-41

Verses 35 - 41

In this set of verses, we meet the first two disciples, Andrew and Simon Peter. It was Andrew that announced to his brother Simon that the Mashiach[5] has come. In Hebrew and in Greek, Mashiach and Christos, mean the same thing: "anointed one." This Man was the "anointed one" of God; the One who was sent to save man.

The disciples addressed Yeshua as "Rabbi." This is a Hebrew term which translates to "teacher." The King James version and some other English versions translate the word as "master." Yeshua notices them following Him and asks them what it is that they seek. The disciples respond by asking Yeshua where He was staying. Yeshua brings them to where He was staying, and the disciples decide to remain with Him. One can only imagine what Yeshua's followers must have felt when they found the One who they had heard and read about all their lives. Now they had not only found Him but were having personal dialogue with Him. Learning from the Messiah Himself, in person, would be an emotion that likely could not be expressed in any dialect.

---

[5] Mashiach (Mah-shee-akh) is Hebrew for Messiah, Christos is the word in Greek.

And he brought him to Jesus. And when Jesus beheld him, He said, Thou art Simon the son of Jona: thou shalt be called Cephas, which is by interpretation, A stone.

The day following Jesus would go forth into Galilee, and findeth Philip, and saith unto him, Follow me.

Now Philip was of Bethsaida, the city of Andrew and Peter. Philip findeth Nathanael, and saith unto him, We have found Him, of whom Moses in the law, and the prophets, did write, Jesus of Nazareth, the son of Joseph.

And Nathanael said unto him, Can there any good thing come out of Nazareth? Philip saith unto him, Come and see. Jesus saw Nathanael coming to Him, and saith of him, Behold an Israelite indeed, in whom is no guile!

Nathanael saith unto Him, Whence knowest thou me? Jesus answered and said unto him, Before that Philip called thee, when thou wast under the fig tree, I saw thee. Nathanael answered and saith unto him, Rabbi, thou art the Son of God; thou art the King of Israel.

Jesus answered and said unto him, Because I said unto thee, I saw thee under the fig tree, believest thou? thou shalt see greater things than these.

And he saith unto him, Verily, verily, I say unto you, Hereafter ye shall see heaven open, and the angels of God ascending and descending upon the Son of man.

John 1: 42-51

Verses 42 - 51

In order to understand the calling of the disciples, let us take a trip back into first century Judaism. During that time, it was expected that a young man did his schooling until his Bar mitzvah (at age 13), at which time he would be sent to live with a person of a specific trade in order to learn that skill. We see this with the apostle Paul as he grew up studying with Rabbi Gamaliel (Acts 22:3). Most rabbis at that time would take disciples who would also work a job on the side as well. Again, we see this example with Paul (Acts 18:1-3, 20:33-35).

In verses 45-46, Phillip finds his brother Nathaniel and announces to him that the Messiah has come. Nathaniel's response was of unbelief, as he questions the place from which Yeshua came (Nazareth). Phillip then tells his brother to see for himself. As Nathaniel approaches Yeshua, Yeshua engages him. Nathaniel is immediately stunned and wonders how this Man he just met for the first time, knows him. As Yeshua begins to give specific details concerning Nathaniel, the realization of who Yeshua is overtakes him. The result of this first encounter results in Nathaniel's confession of faith in Yeshua.

The next item of significance in these verses is the number of disciples that Yeshua chose, namely, twelve. There are some commentators that believe and teach that the biblical number twelve symbolizes perfection. The number twelve has a significance to it as it is seen in various parts of Scripture. For example, Jacob's twelve sons, the twelve tribes of Israel, the twelve gates of the New Jerusalem, and the twelve types of fruits of the Tree of Life (Revelation 22: 2). Based upon these examples, it would seem that there was a numerical significance in Yeshua's calling of twelve disciples. It was not random or happenstance, for the Lord has a reason and specific purpose for everything, even in numbers.

The next thing to take notice of is the type and class of men that the Messiah chose. Yeshua did not choose Israel's most learned biblical scholars and theologians, but rather a collective group of common working men, who in many respects were no different than the male blue-collar workers of today. These were simple, hard-working men doing their best to make a living, facing many of the same struggles that we do today. Yet after Messiah's ascension, through the work of the Holy Spirit, these men became some of the most powerful preachers and brilliant biblical apologists ever know (Acts 2:14-47, 7:1-53).

As we study the disciples, we see them as ordinary human beings that were chosen by the Lord to do extraordinary things. We then come to two simple understandings. One, the groundwork they laid was truly extraordinary, and two, and most importantly, the work they accomplished was truly the work of God.

John Chapter 2: The Ministry Begins

And the third day there was a marriage in Cana of Galilee; and the mother of Jesus was there:

And both Jesus was called, and His disciples, to the marriage.

And when they wanted wine, the mother of Jesus saith unto Him, They have no wine.

John 2: 1-3

Verses 1 - 3

This chapter opens with an event that many of us still partake in today, a wedding. This was a joyous occasion for not only the bride and groom, but also for the families and friends in attendance. It is interesting to note that according to history, these events would at times go on for sometimes as long as a week. The Scripture account makes it clear that Yeshua and His disciples were invited and present for this joyous occasion.

It is at this celebration in a town known as Cana where the first of many of Messiah's miracles are witnessed. Cana was a small town west of the Sea of Galilee, yet not on the coast; rather, Cana sat midway between the Mediterranean Sea and the Sea of Galilee.

According to these verses, not only was Yeshua and His disciples present, but His mother Mary as well. It would seem that Mary's role was in a serving capacity based upon His mother's reaction to what happened next. During the festivities, a problem arose; the guests were running out of wine. Mary approached Yeshua and made Him aware of the situation. A question is raised here: was Mary aware that Yeshua is the Messiah at this point in time? The answer, we believe, is yes, according to all the Gospel accounts. Notice she comes to Him with the problem as it is happening, knowing that there would be no way to quickly acquire more wine, yet she makes Him aware of the problem nonetheless. We believe she did so knowing clearly who and what He is. *"And the angel said unto her, Fear not, Mary: for thou hast found favour with God. And, behold, thou shalt conceive in thy womb, and bring forth a Son, and shalt call His name Jesus. He shall be great, and shall be called the Son of the Highest: and the Lord God shall give unto Him the throne of His father David: And He shall reign over the house of Jacob for ever; and of His kingdom there shall be no end."* (Luke 1: 30-33)[6]

> Jesus saith unto her, Woman, what have I to do with thee? mine hour is not yet come. His mother saith unto the servants, Whatsoever He saith unto you, do it.
>
> And there were set there six waterpots of stone, after the manner of the purifying of the Jews, containing two or three firkins apiece.
>
> Jesus saith unto them, Fill the waterpots with water. And they filled them up to the brim. And

---

[6] See also Matthew 1:23 for Joseph's encounter regarding the identity of Mary's unborn child.

He saith unto them, Draw out now, and bear unto the governor of the feast. And they bare it.

When the ruler of the feast had tasted the water that was made wine, and knew not whence it was: (but the servants which drew the water knew;) the governor of the feast called the bridegroom, And saith unto him, Every man at the beginning doth set forth good wine; and when men have well drunk, then that which is worse: but thou hast kept the good wine until now.

This beginning of miracles did Jesus in Cana of Galilee, and manifested forth His glory; and His disciples believed on Him.

John 2: 4-11

Verses 4 - 11

The first thing to take note of here is Yeshua's response: "Woman, what have I to do with thee? Mine hour is not yet come." What does Yeshua's response mean? Is He referring to something specific? This response is a prophetic warning of what is to come for Yeshua; the Messiah is referring to His crucifixion (Matthew 27:35, John19:16-18).

Throughout the Gospels, at differing points during His ministry, Yeshua would give warnings of what would happen to Him (Mark 8:31, Luke 9:44). Immediately, Mary instructs the servants to do that which Yeshua says. The servants fill the waterpots with water as Yeshua instructed. Here the Scriptures give us a clear indication of how much wine this miracle produced. A "firkin" was approximately 10.2 gallons, and verse 6 states that there were six of these stone waterpots filled with water and miraculously converted into wine. Given the measurement of a firken, each waterpot held around thirty gallons, which confirms the guest list was large.

Some have raised the question if there is a numerical significance to the number of waterpots being six. There could possibly be, but we have not seen it in any of the commentaries and historical sources we have consulted.

In first century Israel, it was customary at weddings, and some other functions, that best wine was brought out and served first. The reason for this possibly would be that at the beginning of the feast, the blessings and toasts were given. So, the best quality of wine would be used for these ceremonies and customs, while the wine that would follow would be mostly for drinking with the meal.

Once Yeshua converted the water to wine, it was then brought to the governor of the feast. This was usually a close acquaintance of the groom that would have been appointed over the ceremonies.

COULD IT BE THAT THE MIRACLE WINE YESHUA CREATED WAS MORE DELICIOUS BECAUSE *HE* MADE IT?

Why was this wine better than the previous wine? We believe because it was made supernaturally by the One who created the fruits of wines. This can be seen in the very blessing for wine. In Hebrew, we pray, *"Baruch atah ADONAI, ELOHEYNU melech ha'olam, boraa poree haggafen,"* which translated is, "Blessed are You, oh, LORD, our GOD, king of the universe, who has given us the fruit of the vine." This prayer is believed by some to trace back as far as the first Passover (Exodus 12:42-51) and has been part of Jewish liturgy ever since.

In summation, that which is created by the Lord will always be superior to that which man makes. This miracle also showed those present, as well as future readers of this Gospel account, the power of the Messiah over the natural world. The water being supernaturally turned to wine by Yeshua was the first miracle of His Messianic ministry. In verse eleven, the Scripture confirms this, and shows how it also served to solidify the faiths of the disciples.

After this He went down to Capernaum, He, and His mother, and His brethren, and His disciples: and they continued there not many days. And the Jews' passover was at hand, and Jesus went up to Jerusalem. And found in the temple those that sold oxen and sheep and doves, and the changers of money sitting: And when He had made a scourge of small cords, He drove them all out of the temple, and the sheep, and the oxen; and poured out the changers' money, and overthrew the tables; And said unto them that sold doves, Take these things hence; make not my Father's house an house of merchandise.

And his disciples remembered that it was written, The zeal of thine house hath eaten me up.

John 2: 12-17

Verses 12 - 17

After the miracle in Cana, Yeshua, His immediate family, and the disciples traveled up to a city on the western shore of the Galilee called Capernaum. However, they did not stay for a significant amount of time. Passover had arrived, and the Jewish people would make their way to Jerusalem to attend and participate in this Feast of the LORD.

John 2: 12-17 describes the account of Yeshua cleansing the temple of the moneychangers. It is important to note that the apostle John records this event at the beginning of Yeshua's Messianic ministry, whereas the synoptic Gospels (Matthew, Mark, and Luke) put this event at the last week of Yeshua's life. Why would this be? Following the content and chronology of John's gospel as well as the others, it would seem that the Messiah cleansed the temple on two occasions, one at the early part of His ministry and then a second at the end. The second would have been the one that lead to His death.

Other commentators aside from ourselves have come to the same conclusion, and we are satisfied based upon our studies, after all, Jewish people traveled to Jerusalem for Feats of the LORD multiple times a year.

Why did Yeshua feel such a need? What caused Him to become so angry at the moneychangers and livestock merchants? Much of it has to do with the animals and those offering them for sale.

The selling of animals for sacrifices was a direct violation of God's law. Why? Because animals that were to be used for temple sacrificial purposes were to be raised and offered by the individuals that raised them. These sacrificial animals were also to be the choicest from the individual's flock or herd, without defect or blemish, as commanded in the Torah. Unrighteous practices described in Jewish historical documents reveal how temple officials would often cheat the weary travelers who came a long way to Jerusalem and trick them into exchanging their "home-grown" sacrificial animal for one of their own. What was happening at the temple at this time was not only wrong but abhorrent, thus became another fulfillment of Messianic prophecy in the Tanakh (Psalm 69:9). Just as Yeshua fulfilled all other Messianic prophecies concerning His first coming, so He fulfilled this as well.

Then answered the Jews and said unto Him, What sign shewest thou unto us, seeing that thou doest these things?

Jesus answered and said unto them, Destroy this temple, and in three days I will raise it up.

Then said the Jews, Forty and six years was this temple in building, and wilt thou rear it up in three days? But He spake of the temple of His body.

John 2: 12-17

Verses 18 - 21

After Yeshua cleansed His Father's house (the temple), His actions caught the attention of the religious leaders who challenged Yeshua, demanding a sign that could prove His authority to do such a thing in the temple. Yeshua's response stuns them as He tells them to destroy "this house" and it will be restored in three days' time. The religious leaders thought He was referring to the actual temple itself, so they could not fathom such a thing.

On the contrary, it must be noted that given who

Yeshua is, it would be more than possible for Him to be able to do exactly that (John 1:1-14). It is clear that the leaders did not understand the context of Yeshua's response, as He was speaking prophetically, referring to His own death, burial, and resurrection (John 19:16-20:10).

In the religious leaders' lack of understanding Yeshua's response, they answer Him by describing the duration of time it took to rebuild the second temple, "forty and six years." Given the duration of time it took to complete the construction, it is easy to imagine the size and magnificence of the second temple. History and archeology reveal that Herod was an exceptional architect. The awe of this incredible building can be seen in the disciples' statement to Yeshua when they left the temple and ascended the Mount of Olives where Yeshua gave His detailed sermon concerning the last days. *"Jesus left the temple area and was going on His way when His disciples came up to Him to call His attention to the [magnificent and massive] buildings of the temple* (Matthew 24:1-2, AMP). Ultimately, Yeshua was describing His body as the temple.

When therefore He was risen from the dead, His disciples remembered that He had said this unto them; and they believed the scripture, and the word which Jesus had said.

Now when He was in Jerusalem at the passover, in the feast day, many believed in His name, when they saw the miracles which He did. But Jesus did not commit himself unto them, because He knew all men, And needed not that any should testify of man: for He knew what was in man.

John 2: 22-25

Verses 22 - 25

As chapter two comes to a close, the Gospel writer jumps ahead in chronology and reflects on events after the second and final cleansing of the temple, as can be seen in verse twenty-two. When Yeshua rose from the grave and showed Himself to the disciples, the disciples recalled that the Lord had told them these things well before it happened (Matthew 16:21, Mark 8:31).

John Chapter 3: Salvation and Regeneration

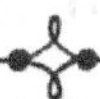

> There was a man of the Pharisees, named Nicodemus, a ruler of the Jews: The same came to Jesus by night, and said unto Him, Rabbi, we know that thou art a teacher come from God: for no man can do these miracles that thou doest, except God be with him.
>
> John 3: 1-2

Verses 1 - 2

John chapter three is probably one of the most well-known chapters, from the famous 3:16 passage that Hollywood likes to satire, to the Messiah's explanation regarding the need to be born again. In our estimation, John chapter three is of great theological importance due to its emphasis on what is necessary to gain eternal life.

In the first two verses, a Pharisee by the name of Nicodemus (a member of the religious leadership of Israel as well as a Rabbi, himself) met with Yeshua by night. Why at night? Most likely out of concern of what his fellow Rabbis would think about such a meeting; Yeshua was under Pharisaical scrutiny, and not in a good way.

Notice Nicodemus's confession at this encounter; he addresses Him as "Rabbi." This is significant because one of the chief Rabbis of first century Israel acknowledged Yeshua as a rabbinical equal. Was Messiah recognized as a Rabbi by the religious authorities? According to Scripture, yes. We see examples of this throughout the Gospels. As in, *"And Jesus went about all Galilee, **teaching in their synagogues**, and preaching the gospel of the kingdom, and healing all manner of sickness and all manner of disease among the people."* (Matthew 4:23)[7]

Yeshua "taught in the synagogues." He would not have been able to do this unless he was recognized as an

---

[7] See also Luke 4:16-37.

official Rabbi. Furthermore, did you catch a subtle clue when Nicodemus said, "…we know that thou art a teacher come from God."? The "we" indicates that not only did Nicodemus recognize Yeshua's status, but at least a portion of his fellow Jewish leaders did as well.

> Jesus answered and said unto him, Verily, verily, I say unto thee, Except a man be born again, he cannot see the kingdom of God.
>
> Nicodemus saith unto Him, How can a man be born when he is old? can he enter the second time into his mother's womb, and be born?
>
> Jesus answered, Verily, verily, I say unto thee, Except a man be born of water and of the Spirit, he cannot enter into the kingdom of God.
>
> John 3: 3-5

Verses 3 - 5

In a world of liberal clergy and compromising pastors who no long hold to nor preach that salvation is the only access to heaven, verses such as these make it absolutely clear that the unsaved will not enter the kingdom of God. Notice Yeshua's response, "Verily, verily, I say unto thee, Except a man be born again, he cannot see the kingdom of God". Without being born again (being saved), there is no other access in to God's kingdom. Yeshua is the only source of this salvation, which means He is the only access to God and His kingdom, as we see again a bit later in John's Gospel (John 14:6). Salvation as the only means to enter into the kingdom, and Yeshua as the only source of salvation is the core of John's theology and an essential doctrine of Scripture. There is no other savior and no other god who can save but the Lord Himself, as we see in the book of Isaiah the prophet, *"Thus saith the Lord the King of Israel, and his redeemer the Lord of hosts; I am the first, and I am the last; and beside Me there is no God."* (Isaiah 44:6). Amen!

> That which is born of the flesh is flesh; and that which is born of the Spirit is spirit. Marvel not that I said unto thee, Ye must be born again. The wind bloweth where it listeth, and thou hearest the sound thereof, but canst not tell whence it cometh, and whither it goeth: so is every one that is born of the Spirit.
>
> John 3: 6-8

Verses 6 - 8

Here we have the clear and distinct difference between natural birth and spiritual birth. Natural birth is exactly that, a mother gives physical birth to an infant. Spiritual birth is when an individual repents and believes in Yeshua as Adonai (Lord) and Mashiach (Messiah/savior), and thus, is forgiven and saved (Acts 16:31). That which is of natural birth is of mankind, but that which is born again is of God and His will. *"Neither is there salvation in any other: for there is none other name under heaven given among men, whereby we must be saved."* (Acts 4:12)

In verse 8, the Lord illustrates the difference by the unpredictability of wind. Natural birth can be predicted by duration of time of pregnancy of a mother, where a spiritual birth can happen at any time to an individual at any age when he or she realizes their sins, repents, and accepts the Lord Yeshua by faith. At any time, in any place, anyone can come to the realization that they are a sinner before God, that they need a savior, and accept Yeshua for forgiveness of sin that leads to eternal life.

> Nicodemus answered and said unto Him, How can these things be?
>
> Jesus answered and said unto him, Art thou a master of Israel, and knowest not these things? Verily, verily, I say unto thee, We speak that we do know, and testify that we have seen; and ye receive not our witness.
>
> John 3: 9-11

Verses 9 - 11

Yeshua responds to Nicodemus's questions with a counter question: "Art thou a master of Israel, and knowest not these things?" Is this the Lord responding in sarcasm or being degrading? Not at all. Yeshua was getting this chief rabbi to *think*, given his position in the community. Here is a man who has made his life's pursuit in the study of Holy Scripture and Jewish theology yet has never heard of these biblical teachings. Why? Wasn't salvation taught in the Tanakh (the only Scriptures they had at the time)? And if so, wouldn't a learned rabbi like Nicodemus have been familiar with it?

Absolutely, salvation was taught in the Old

Testament. Both Moses and King David spoke of salvation. *"The Lord is my strength and song, and he is become my* **salvation***: he is my God, and I will prepare him an habitation; my father's God, and I will exalt him."* (Exodus 15:2), and *"Restore unto me the joy of thy* **salvation***; and uphold me with thy free spirit."* (Psalm 51: 12) are two of many examples.

As for the second issue, why didn't Nicodemus know this if he was a scholar, Yeshua's counter question is not sarcasm, but convicting. As in, how is it (Nicodemus) that you are a teacher and theologian of Israel who has spent his life studying God's word, studying the sages' writings on God's word, and still not know these things? Furthermore, could this gentle chastisement from the Messiah be something that Nicodemus reflects on later, as a full-fledged believer? Afterall, it occurred with the disciples: *"These things understood not His disciples at the first:* **but when Jesus was glorified, then remembered** *they that these things were written of Him, and that they had done these things unto Him."* (John 12: 16)

> If I have told you earthly things, and ye believe not, how shall ye believe, if I tell you of heavenly things? And no man hath ascended up to heaven, but He that came down from heaven, even the Son of man which is in heaven. And as Moses lifted up the serpent in the wilderness, even so must the Son of man be lifted up: That whosoever believeth in Him should not perish, but have eternal life.
>
> John 3: 12-15

Verses 12 - 15

In verse 12, Yeshua explains, if Nicodemus could not understand things of the world he and others lived in, how would he be able to comprehend the things not of the physical world (heaven)? Humans, with our finite minds, have a problem believing and understanding the infinite and eternal. This is evident later in John's Gospel with Thomas after Yeshua's resurrection: *"But Thomas, one of the twelve, called Didymus, was not with them when Jesus came. The other disciples therefore said unto him, We have seen the Lord. But he said unto them, Except I shall see in his hands the print of the nails, and put my finger into the print of the nails, and thrust my hand into his side, I will not believe."* (John 20:24-25)

In verse 13, the Lord points out that there has never been anyone that has been taken up to heaven from our world. This is referring to Yeshua in the book of Acts where after His resurrection, He was lifted up and ascended into heaven (Acts 1:9-10). Because He is from heaven, only He can ascend back into heaven *alive*.

It must be noted that during the tribulation, after the two witnesses are murdered by the antichrist enforcers, they are resurrected and ascend up into heaven alive in front of many (Revelation 11:11-12). Does this mean there is a contradiction in God's written Word? Absolutely not! Up unto that point in the future, no man had or has ascended alive into heaven. When this event occurs during the tribulation period, it happens, by God's will and power alone.

Next, Yeshua points out that He must be "lifted up". He must be the top priority of faith, the one to be looked up to and believed. The illustration He uses is how Moses lifted a certain staff when the fiery serpents were sent upon the Jewish people as a judgment (Numbers 21: 4-9). All those who looked upon the lifted staff were saved (from snakebite, thus death). All those who did not were killed by the snakes. This is more evidence of God's grace and mercy. The people sinned, God sent the serpents, the people complained, and God sent relief, commanding Moses to make a brass serpent set upon a pole. If anyone was bitten, they could look upon the serpent on the pole and live (Numbers 21:4-9). This is and was a picture of Yeshua, the one who is to be lifted up (literally as in the crucifixion and figuratively as the King of kings[8] and the Name above all names), who came from heaven, and will ascend back to heaven. He is the One who gives eternal life (V:15). This is what Yeshua was explaining to Nicodemus.

> For God so loved the world, that He gave His only begotten Son, that whosoever believeth in him should not perish, but have everlasting life.
>
> John 3: 16

Verse 16

This is probably one of the most well-known verses of the Holy Bible, both by the believing and unbelieving world. To the unbelieving world, this verse is, sadly, nothing more

---

[8] Revelation 17: 14.

than a catch phrase attached to a guy wearing it as a sign in a movie. However, to the believer, it is a verse of great hope and part of the foundation of our faith.

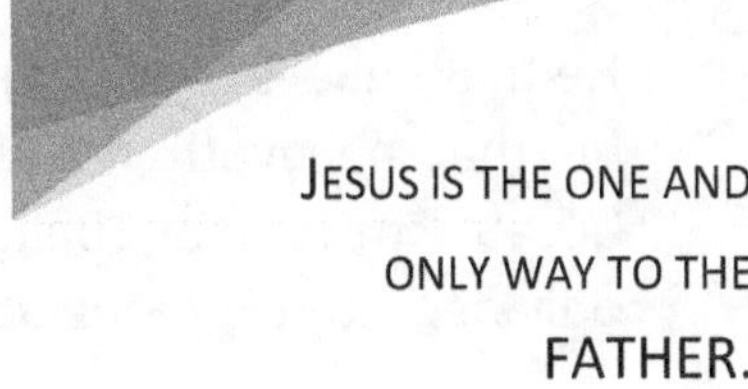

The great British theologian of the 1800s, Charles Spurgeon, once said, "John 3:16 serves as a thesis statement for the Christian's faith."[9] Believing on the only begotten Son of God, who is none other than Yeshua, (Matthew 3:17, 17:5), gives a repented and believing person eternal life in heaven. Belief on the only begotten Son of God assures the believer that when they die, they will not perish in eternal hell, which is the inevitable consequence for rejecting God's only Son (Revelation 21:8). Here, the offer for salvation is given because of God's love to whosoever will believe the Gospel and receive it.

---

[9] Find the entire sermon, *Immeasurable Love*, John 3:16, at
https://www.spurgeon.org/resource-library/sermons/immeasurable-love .

For God sent not His Son into the world to condemn the world; but that the world through Him might be saved.

He that believeth on Him is not condemned: but he that believeth not is condemned already, because he hath not believed in the name of the only begotten Son of God.

And this is the condemnation, that light is come into the world, and men loved darkness rather than light, because their deeds were evil.

For every one that doeth evil hateth the light, neither cometh to the light, lest his deeds should be reproved.

But he that doeth truth cometh to the light, that his deeds may be made manifest, that they are wrought in God.

John 3: 17-21

Verses 17 - 21

God's purpose in sending His only Son Yeshua into the world was not for the purpose of condemnation, but to save the lost. Again, these verses confirm what several other verses make clear, that salvation only comes through Yeshua, who is God's only begotten Son. Those who reject the salvation that comes through Yeshua are condemned.

Furthermore, these verses reveal the sad truth of the fallen nature of humanity. Yeshua is the Light of the world, as we read at the beginning of John's Gospel (John 1:4-5). The Light came into a world that was plunged into darkness from the fall into sin (Genesis 3), and because mankind is immersed in that darkness, it does not understand the Light, which is Messiah Yeshua. To those who receive the Light have the inclination to do what is good in the sight of God, but those who reject the Light will do (and continue to do) evil and all that is contrary to God.

It is logical; those who accept the Light will do what is good in the sight of God because of the Light inside them. Only the Light that came from God can rescue mankind from the darkness of this world.

> After these things came Jesus and His disciples into the land of Judaea; and there he tarried with them, and baptized. And John also was baptizing in Aenon near to Salim, because there was much water there: and they came, and were baptized. For John was not yet cast into prison.

Then there arose a question between some of John's disciples and the Jews about purifying. And they came unto John, and said unto him, Rabbi, he that was with thee beyond Jordan, to whom thou barest witness, behold, the same baptizeth, and all men come to him.

John 3: 22-26

Verses 22 - 26

We now come to the testimony of John the baptizer. At this point in time, John had amassed a very large following even though John's preaching and teachings all pointed to and were about Yeshua, not John himself. Both Yeshua, His disciples, John, and those who were following him, were in the region of Judea. This was prior to the arrest and unjust execution of John the Baptist (Luke 3:18-20, Matthew 14:1-14).

John answered and said, A man can receive nothing, except it be given him from heaven. Ye yourselves bear me witness, that I said, I am not the Christ, but that I am sent before Him.

He that hath the bride is the bridegroom: but the friend of the bridegroom, which standeth and heareth him, rejoiceth greatly because of the bridegroom's voice: this my joy therefore is fulfilled. He must increase, but I must decrease.

He that cometh from above is above all: he that is of the earth is earthly, and speaketh of the earth: he that cometh from heaven is above all.

And what he hath seen and heard, that he testifieth; and no man receiveth his testimony. He that hath received his testimony hath set to his seal that God is true. For he whom God hath sent speaketh the words of God: for God giveth not the Spirit by measure unto him.

The Father loveth the Son, and hath given all things into his hand.

Verses 27 - 35

Again, we again see the humble nature of John, as he stated, "He must increase, but I must decrease." (v:30) A true preacher must not be seeking attention and recognition for himself but needs to get his listeners to recognize and follow the Messiah Yeshua. Said another way, all preachers should encourage their hearers to believe the Word of God, not their personal opinions.

He that believeth on the Son hath everlasting life: and he that believeth not the Son shall not see life; but the wrath of God abideth on him.

John 3: 36

Verse 36

The baptizer closes out his testimony with the foundation of faith and essential theology of salvation: belief on the only Son of God, who is none other than Yeshua, brings eternal life. Rejecting Yeshua as God's only Son and Messiah brings the consequence of God's wrath, which is eternal punishment. It is not God's desire for anyone to face such an eternity, which is why He gave His only begotten Son, Yeshua, out of His love (v:16). The choice of believing on Yeshua and the eternal hope of heaven that comes with that belief is what God desires of all people.

John Chapter 4: A Woman at a Well & a Nobleman's Son

When therefore the Lord knew how the Pharisees had heard that Jesus made and baptized more disciples than John, (Though Jesus Himself baptized not, but His disciples,). He left Judaea, and departed again into Galilee. And He must needs go through Samaria. Then cometh He to a city of Samaria, which is called Sychar, near to the parcel of ground that Jacob gave to his son Joseph. Now Jacob's well was there.

Jesus therefore, being wearied with His journey, sat thus on the well: and it was about the sixth hour. There cometh a woman of Samaria to draw water: Jesus saith unto her, Give Me to drink. (For His disciples were gone away unto the city to buy meat.)

> Then saith the woman of Samaria unto Him, How is it that thou, being a Jew, askest drink of me, which am a woman of Samaria? for the Jews have no dealings with the Samaritans.
>
> John 4: 1-9

Verses 1 - 9

At this stage in Yeshua's ministry, His following exceeded that of John the Baptizer. These new followers of the Messiah not only came to faith and believed, but also received immersion (baptism). Verse two is a side note to let the readers know that these new disciples were not baptized by the Lord Yeshua, but by His (original) disciples.

Yeshua and the apostles are now departing Judea (the southern region of Israel) and heading back toward the region of Galilee. On the way, Yeshua states that there is a priority to pass through Samaria ("And he must needs go through Samariah."). The context of this would indicate a divine reason rather than a practical one, to specifically pass through the area.

Samariah (named "Sebaste" by Herod shortly before

the first century) is a region between Galilee and Jerusalem. The people of Samariah were at spiritual odds with the Jewish people in Judea. The Samaritan Jews had intermarried with Gentiles centuries before (as 2 Kings 17 shows), but the animosity of the Judean Jews toward the Samaritans was not so much of their intermingling with Gentiles, but the fact that they did so with Israel's enemies. Specifically, Assyrians and Babylonians, two Gentile nations that invaded Israel and destroyed the holy city Jerusalem and the temple of Solomon. The other reason for Jewish animosity was the Samaritans belief that God ordained Mount Gerizim for sacrifices, not Jerusalem, and this rift that lasted centuries.

As Yeshua and His disciples came into Samaria, they entered a city called Sychar, which was formally Shechem. The verse states it was the "sixth hour," which is 12 PM in modern time, and the hottest part of the day. They arrived at the place the patriarch Jacob gave to his son Joseph (Genesis 33:19). Yeshua goes to the well of Jacob and following was a Samaritan woman. When the woman arrived, Yeshua requests of her water from the well. This is also an example of Yeshua's humanity. While He is God in the form of flesh, he was also human and experienced the things of humanity, such as fatigue and thirst.[10] The woman's response demonstrates the feelings between the Samaritans and the Jews of that day.

> Jesus answered and said unto her, If thou knewest the gift of God, and who it is that saith to thee, Give Me to drink; thou wouldest have asked of Him, and He would have given thee living water.
>
> The woman saith unto Him, Sir, thou hast nothing to draw with, and the well is deep: from whence then hast thou that living water? Art thou greater than our father Jacob, which gave us the well, and drank thereof himself, and his children, and his cattle?
>
> Jesus answered and said unto her, Whosoever drinketh of this water shall thirst again: But whosoever drinketh of the water that I shall give him shall never thirst; but the water that I shall give him shall be in him a well of water springing up into everlasting life.
>
> John 4: 10-14

---

[10] This is also evident later, in the crucifixion account, at John 19:16.

Verses 10 - 14

In an encrypted fashion, Yeshua begins to reveal who He is. *"If thou knewest the gift of God, and who it is that saith to thee, Give me to drink; thou wouldest have asked of him, and he would have given thee living water."* (v:10) This statement reveals Yeshua as the Messiah as well as the gift of salvation He offers. The woman wonders how it is that He is offering her water, when it is Yeshua's hands are empty and He has nothing to draw out water from the well.

Next, the Samaritan woman asks Yeshua directly if He is someone greater than the patriarch and founder of that town. It is here that Yeshua reveals the water that He is referring to is not the earthly water, rather He is referencing salvation and eternal life, the living waters that flow in the Kingdom (Revelation 22:1-2). If the Samaritan woman understood at this point Yeshua's true identity, she would have realized that the Man at the well is greater than Jacob; that Yeshua comes eternal life.

The woman saith unto Him, Sir, give me this water, that I thirst not, neither come hither to draw.

Jesus saith unto her, Go, call thy husband, and come hither.

The woman answered and said, I have no husband. Jesus said unto her, Thou hast well said, I have no husband: For thou hast had five husbands; and he whom thou now hast is not thy husband: in that saidst thou truly.

The woman saith unto him, Sir, I perceive that thou art a prophet.

John 4: 15-19

Verses 15 - 19

The Lord is now going to show to the woman who He is by revealing her need for repentance and salvation. He begins by telling the woman to call for her husband, knowing already what she most likely considered personal and private. Notice that when Yeshua explained that she had had many husbands, he did so in a very compassionate fashion. He did not accuse nor chastise her, and when He said these things, he did so in the company of just the two of them, not in front of the apostles or anyone in the village. While the Lord is righteous judge (Revelation 20:11-15), He is also a compassionate savior.

In verse 19, the woman reveals that she knows enough Scripture to recognize the prophetic aspects of the coming Messiah, that when He comes, He will be a prophet (Deuteronomy 18:15).

> Our fathers worshipped in this mountain; and ye say, that in Jerusalem is the place where men ought to worship.
>
> Jesus saith unto her, Woman, believe Me, the hour cometh, when ye shall neither in this mountain, nor yet at Jerusalem, worship the Father. Ye worship ye know not what: we know what we worship: for salvation is of the Jews. But the hour cometh, and now is, when the true worshippers shall worship the Father in spirit and in truth: for the Father seeketh such to worship him.
>
> John 4: 20-23

Verses 20 - 23

By the statement the woman now poses to Yeshua, it is clear that she is aware that He is a prophet of Israel. Her response is not surprising, given that they had not met before and He knew every detail of her current and previous relationships.

The woman points out the Samaritan tradition of worship being offered at Mount Gerezim instead of Mount Moriah (the Temple Mount) in Jerusalem. Prior to Mount Moriah being the chosen spot for the Beit Hamiqdash (The Temple), the most holy mountain would have been Mount Sinai, where God spoke to Moses and gave His most holy law (Exodus 19-20).

Yeshua informs her that there will be a time when the worship of God will no longer be a designated place on earth. Yeshua is referring to His crucifixion, what would happen at His last breath. It is important to understand this in context. Yeshua is not saying that physical places appointed in Scripture will lose their significance, rather believers will accept His salvation and then worship God in spirit, any time, in any place. Remember, as stated in Matthew 18:20, wherever believers come together to pray and worship in fellowship, the Lord's presence is there, no matter where they may be physically.

> God is a Spirit: and they that worship Him must worship Him in spirit and in truth.
>
> John 4: 24

Verse 24

What does this mean, worship in "spirit and in truth"? Worship offered in spirit occurs only when your spirit is united with Yeshua through faith. Likewise, worship offered in truth can only be in Truth **because** the Spirit of God lives within you. Stated plainly in this verse: *God is a Spirit*. His Spirit resides in those who believe on Yeshua for salvation (1 John 5:6-7).

This most wonderful mystery comes up in John chapter 14, where Yeshua said to His disciples (and by extension, you and me), *"If you love Me, keep My commands. And I will ask the Father, and He will give you another Advocate to help you and be with you forever— **the Spirit of truth**. The world cannot accept Him, because it neither sees Him nor knows Him. But you know Him, **for He lives with you and will be in you**."* (John 14: 15-17)

This is the worship that God desires, a heart that cries

out to Him and does so in complete faith and sincerity. As the Psalmist wrote, *"Open my lips, Lord, and my mouth will declare Your praise You do not delight in sacrifice, or I would bring it; You do not take pleasure in burnt offerings. My sacrifice, O God, is a broken spirit; a broken and contrite heart You, God, will not despise.* (Psalm 51: 15-17)

> The woman saith unto Him, I know that Messias cometh, which is called Christ: when He is come, He will tell us all things.
>
> Jesus saith unto her, I that speak unto thee am He.
>
> John 4: 25-26

Verses 25 - 26

"I that speak unto thee am He." In no uncertain terms, Yeshua just identified Himself as the Messiah. His statement is deliberate and direct; Yeshua wanted the woman to know that He was the One she spoke of, the Mashiach that had been prophesied to come and "tell all things."

Furthermore, this statement is also not only important theologically, but apologetically as well, because over the centuries, numerous liberal clergy, academics, and opposing religions claim, "Nowhere in Scripture does Jesus say He is the Messiah." Right here, from His own mouth, Yeshua's declaration is clear, He is the expected Messiah that the prophets spoke of in the Tanakh! (Deuteronomy 18:15, Is 53:5, 61:1,2)

> And upon this came His disciples, and marvelled that He talked with the woman: yet no man said, What seekest thou? or, Why talkest thou with her?
>
> The woman then left her waterpot, and went her way into the city, and saith to the men, Come, see a man, which told me all things that ever I did: is not this the Christ?
>
> John 4: 27-29

Verses 27-29

It was at this time his disciples returned to Yeshua after a brief outing to purchase food and provisions. They marveled to find Him speaking to a Samaritan woman, alone at the well. In those day, it was not customary for a rabbi to speak one on one with a woman at all, much less one from Samaria. The Greek word used for marvel is "thaumazo" which means "astonished," which fits this context well. Although not stated directly, what if the Lord purposefully waited for his brethren to leave before he engaged the woman, knowing what their reactions would be? As it was, He was able to speak with the Samaritan woman uninterrupted.

In verse 29, woman returns to her village and announces to the men who she met and asked them to come and see for themselves. Does she believe Yeshua is the Messiah? Her response to the locals makes her position clear, *"Come, see a man, which told me all things that ever I did: is this not the Christ?"* The confession isn't so much an affirmation that He is, but rather, how could He *not be* the Christ?

> Then they went out of the city, and came unto Him. In the mean while His disciples prayed Him, saying, Master, eat.
>
> But He said unto them, I have meat to eat that ye know not of.
>
> Therefore said the disciples one to another, Hath any man brought Him ought to eat?

> Jesus saith unto them, My meat is to do the will of Him that sent Me, and to finish His work. Say not ye, There are yet four months, and then cometh harvest? behold, I say unto you, Lift up your eyes, and look on the fields; for they are white already to harvest. And he that reapeth receiveth wages, and gathereth fruit unto life eternal: that both he that soweth and he that reapeth may rejoice together. And herein is that saying true, One soweth, and another reapeth. I sent you to reap that whereon ye bestowed no labour: other men laboured, and ye are entered into their labours.
>
> John 4: 30-38

Verses 30 - 38

Upon the disciples return, they urged Yeshua to eat. It could be that after seeing the Lord break rabbinic protocol by conversing with a woman in private, they thought maybe He did so as a result of extreme hunger and fatigue, due to their recent long journey. For whatever reason, Yeshua takes the opportunity to turn their concern into a teaching occasion.

The Lord conveys to His disciples that His food is to do all that the Father has sent Him to do. The Messianic mission is to fulfill the Tanakh, meaning, all the prophecies concerning His first coming are to be carried out completely. The "meat to eat" that the disciples do not yet know will be His arrest, crucifixion, death, burial, resurrection, and ascension (Isaiah 53:4-9, Daniel 9:26, Psalm 110:1 Matthew 26:47-28:10, Acts 1:6-11).

Yeshua's food is to carry out His Messianic mission until it is complete, thus everything the prophets foretold concerning Messiah's first coming. When Yeshua returns, His food will be to carry out everything the prophets and apostles wrote that Messiah would do at His second coming, thus completely fulfilling the second part of His Messianic mission. This will also include teaching and sending His disciples out to bring others to the faith.

Read Yeshua's words in another translation: *"My food,"* said Jesus, *"is to do the will of him who sent me and to finish his work. Don't you have a saying, 'It's still four months until harvest'? I tell you, open your eyes and look at the fields! They are ripe for harvest. Even now the one who reaps draws a wage and harvests a crop for eternal life, so that the sower and the reaper may be glad together. Thus the saying 'One sows and another reaps' is true. I sent you to reap what you have not worked for.*

Others have done the hard work, and you have reaped the benefits of their labor." (John 4: 34-38 NIV)

The prophets of old foretold the Messiah and "did the hard work" that the disciples (and all of us) can benefit from!

> And many of the Samaritans of that city believed on Him for the saying of the woman, which testified, He told me all that ever I did. So when the Samaritans were come unto Him, they besought Him that He would tarry with them: and He abode there two days. And many more believed because of His own word;
>
> And said unto the woman, Now we believe, not because of thy saying: for we have heard Him ourselves, and know that this is indeed the Christ, the Saviour of the world.
>
> John 4: 39-42

Verses 39 - 42

The result of Yeshua's interaction with the Samaritan woman, many people in that village came to hear Him, and many of those came to faith. Here was a people the Jews views as apostates, and now these same people became believers in Israel's Messiah. God's love extends to all who will hear, receive, and believe on God's Anointed; all these will receive the reward of salvation.

Another undeniable statement from these Samaritan villagers occurs in verse 42. They come to the knowledge that Yeshua is the Messiah, the "Savior of the world." Not because of what the woman told them, but because they went down to meet Him and saw and heard for themselves.

> Now after two days He departed thence, and went into Galilee. For Jesus Himself testified, that a prophet hath no honour in His own country.

Verse 43 - 44

Yeshua and His disciples spent two days in the Samaritan village before making their way back to the Galilean region. Yeshua makes a proverbial statement concerning how a prophet is not honored in his own country. What did He mean by this? He may have been referring to how the prophets of the past were treated by their own countrymen, for example the fate of Isaiah (Hebrews 11:37), or how the people turned on Moses (Numbers 16:1-25). Also, He could have been speaking prophetically regarding His own future to come at His crucifixion.

A look at Matthew's account of Yeshua visiting Galilee reveals He meant all of these together. The people in His hometown knew Him as a boy, would have seen Him growing up, they knew His parents, His siblings, and this was a hard thing for them to forget when the people around them were believing he was the Messiah.[11]

"Coming to His hometown, He began teaching the people in their synagogue, and they were amazed. 'Where did this Man get this wisdom and these miraculous powers?" they asked. "Isn't this the carpenter's son? Isn't His mother's name Mary, and aren't His brothers James, Joseph, Simon and Judas? Aren't all His sisters with us? Where then did this Man get all these things?" And they took offense at Him. But Jesus said to them, "A prophet is not without honor except in His own town and in His own home." And he did not do many miracles there because of their lack of faith." (Matthew 13: 54-58 NIV)

---

[11] Joseph (Matthew 1: 20-21) and Mary (Luke 1: 30-33) knew who He was, and that was enough for God's purposes!

Then when He was come into Galilee, the Galilaeans received Him, having seen all the things that He did at Jerusalem at the feast: for they also went unto the feast.

So Jesus came again into Cana of Galilee, where He made the water wine. And there was a certain nobleman, whose son was sick at Capernaum.

When he heard that Jesus was come out of Judaea into Galilee, he went unto Him, and besought Him that He would come down, and heal his son: for he was at the point of death.

Then said Jesus unto him, Except ye see signs and wonders, ye will not believe.

The nobleman saith unto Him, Sir, come down ere my child die.

Jesus saith unto him, Go thy way; thy son liveth. And the man believed the word that Jesus had spoken unto him, and he went his way. And as he was now going down, his servants met him, and told him, saying, Thy son liveth. Then enquired he of them the hour when he began to amend. And they said unto him, Yesterday at the seventh hour the fever left him. So the father knew that it was at the same hour, in the which

Jesus said unto him, Thy son liveth: and himself believed, and his whole house.

This is again the second miracle that Jesus did, when He was come out of Judaea into Galilee.

(John 4: 45-54)

Verses 45 - 54

The Lord and His disciples are back in Cana where He performed the miracle at the wedding. A local nobleman[12] heard of Yeshua's arrival to the region and came to inquire of Him, because his son was sick and close to death. This was not uncommon, for in first-century Israel, oftentimes sickness did result in death due to treatment limitations of the day. So the nobleman pleads with Yeshua, hoping for the healing power associated with His reputation.

Notice Yeshua's first response in verse 48, *"Except ye see signs and wonders, ye will not believe."* There are many cases in the Gospels and Acts where the people only believed if they saw the miracle for themselves.

A sad part of the fallen nature of man is skepticism

---

[12] The nobleman could have been a religious leader or an officer from Herod's court; the account does not specify.

regarding our faith in God and Yeshua. Such was the case with Thomas after the resurrection. The disciple was not present when Yeshua appeared to the others, risen from the dead, and when told of it, he did not believe their testimony. He said to them, *"Except I shall see in his hands the print of the nails, and put my finger into the print of the nails, and thrust my hand into his side, I will not believe."* (John 20:25) This is not how faith in the Lord is to be; we believe because of His word, and take Him at His Word. As Yeshua said to Thomas appearing to him in His resurrected body, *"Blessed are they that have not seen, and yet have believed."* (John 20:29)

We should believe because of the testimony of Scripture, knowing by faith that it is God's written and spoken Word. And the Holy Spirit inside of us testifies of this to help us believe. *"The Spirit Himself testifies with our spirit that we are God's children."* (Romans 8:16)

So, back to the nobleman, he asked Yeshua to come to his house to heal his son. Yeshua handled the request in a different way. Rather than going to the nobleman's home and physically touching the sick lad, Yeshua simply speaks the sick man's son healed. Why? As the rest of the account goes, after Yeshua spoke the healing, he sent the man home. Almost there, the nobleman's servants meet him and tell him that the fever left his son. The nobleman gets confirmation of the miracle by asking what time the fever left the lad. Why did Yeshua do the healing this way? The answer is in verse 53: *"...the father knew that it was at the same hour in which Jesus said unto him, Thy son liveth: and himself believed, and his whole house."* When the nobleman had confirmation, he then believed, and not only him, but his whole household. This here is more evidence of Yeshua's mercy; this man needed a sign to believe, and Yeshua – knowing this – still healed the boy. This is our God, and his mercy endures forever.

God's blessings to all who read this, in Yeshua's name.

Related Archeology:

Believers in the Bible know that every claim of Scripture is true and take those claims on faith (John 20:29). From God creating the universe out of nothing, to the miraculous parting of the Red Sea (Genesis 1-2, Exodus 14:21-31), to the commandments being written by God's own finger, to the Messiah Yeshua Himself raising from the dead (Exodus 31:18, Matthew 28:5-6), for centuries, Bible believers have taken these accounts as truth from the testimony of the Holy Scriptures.

We believe the accounts in Scripture, and we also believe that God leaves His mark in our human recorded history. For this reason, we include a Biblical archeology section to this commentary. We want to make clear that some of the following historical items we present are still debated by scholars and clergy. At the same time, there have been discoveries of biblical items and places that have been confirmed as legitimate. However, it is also a known fact there have been forgeries of antiquities over the centuries. In the items we are going to present, we give the Scripture accounts of them, but we also encourage you to research and examine the evidence and decide for yourselves.

The Titulus Crucis (Title of The Cross)

First up is the Titulus Crucis. *"And Pilate wrote a title and put it on the cross. And the writing was, JESUS OF NAZARETH THE KING OF THE JEWS. This title then read many of the Jews: for the place where Jesus was crucified was nigh to the city: and it was written in Hebrew, and Greek, and Latin."* (John 19:19-20)

According to the Gospel account of the crucifixion of Yeshua, Pontius Pilate had a title written and placed above the head of the one being executed. History confirms these titles were wooden plaques inscribed with the accused person's name and the crimes they were charged with. The title of Yeshua's cross, known in Latin as The Titulus Crucis, was the plaque nailed to Yeshua's cross the day the Roman's executed Him. When discussing relics of the Church (and archeology in general), one has to be careful, because many relics discovered over the centuries turned out to be forgeries, or they did not line up with Scripture or history. Having said that, let us look at the evidence behind this relic, and see if it is, in fact, the actual title from Yeshua's cross.

The first question to pose when determining its authenticity, does it line up with the Bible's account? Not writings or traditions of the Church, but the Holy Bible itself? As seen at the start of this section and the quote from John 19, yes, it lines up with Scripture. In fact, the title is not only documented in John's gospel, but is also included in the other three Gospel accounts as well.

Above his head they placed the written charge against him: THIS IS JESUS, THE KING OF THE JEWS. (Matthew 27: 37 NIV)

"...The written notice of the charge against him read: THE KING OF THE JEWS." (Mark 15: 26 NIV)

"There was a written notice above him, which read: THIS IS THE KING OF THE JEWS." (Luke 23: 28 NIV)

Photograph of the relic, Titular Crucis. *Photograph Source: Public Domain*

Artist's rendition of relief before the characters were worn off. *Photograph Source: Public Domain*

The next piece of evidence is the Title relic's history. Years ago, the Title was allowed to be carbon-dated and the results showed it to be from the time between the 980's A.D. to the 1000's A.D. This timeframe would make it a relic created during the Crusades. It is no secret that there were a handful of relics made during that time. However, experts in ancient languages and paleography from the Israel Antiquities Authority, Hebrew University, as well as other institutions, put it in the time period of the crucifixion of Yeshua. These experts feel that the Titulus relic may be the actual title that was nailed to Yeshua's cross as the relic's history puts it centuries before the Crusades.

The Titulus relic currently sits at the Santa Croce Church in Italy. The basilica was built on the ruins of empress Helena, Constantine's mother's original house. When Constantine came to power in the 300's A.D., he sent his mother on a mission to Israel to find and retrieve the relics of the time period of the New Testament, specifically to find the cross Yeshua was crucified on. When Helena arrived in Jerusalem, she did not find the actual cross but did come across the Title plaque. From our research, there are differing stories and legends on the matter, depending on the tradition you're studying, as to how she acquired the Title. If this Titulus is the real one, then it only adds strength to New Testament apologetics.

Next, let's look at this parchment that may have been penned by the very earliest Yeshua-believing copyists.

Rylands Papyrus P52

The Rylands Papyrus archived between glass. *Photograph Source: Public Domain*

"Then said Pilate unto them, Take ye Him, and judge Him according to your law. The Jews therefore said unto him, It is not lawful for us to put any man death: That the saying of Jesus might be fulfilled, which He spake, signifying what death He should die. Then Pilate entered into the judgment hall again, and called Jesus, and said unto Him, Art thou the King of the Jews?" (John 18:31-33)

"Pilate therefore said unto Him, Art thou a king then? Jesus answered, Thou sayest I am a king. To this end was I born, and for this cause came I into the world, that I should bear witness unto the truth. Every one that is of the truth heareth my voice. Pilate saith unto him, What is truth? And when he had said this, he went out again unto the Jews, and saith unto them, I find in him no fault at all." (John 18:37-38)

These two passages are the quotes from John's Gospel that are believed to have been on this fragment, except the it is missing much of the wording. This parchment is all that remains of the oldest known copy of John's Gospel. The fragment currently resides at John Rylands University Library in Manchester, UK. The fragment was acquired in

1920 from Egypt by a British Egyptologist named Bernard Grenfell. The fragment was among a group of fragments that were being selected for the library. Dates of the Gospel copy fragment have ranged from as early as 100 AD to as late as the early 300's AD Again, it is important to note that scholars differ on the dating of the copy. However, if the dating of 100 AD or a decade or so after is correct, then is it possible that this may have been the first of a series of copies from the apostle's original writing?

The fragment is written on the front and back side, making the parchment a piece of a page from a bound type book and not from a scroll. We are not paleography experts nor are we experts in ancient languages, but if this fragment is in fact from the early 100's A.D., then what is the possibility that this may have been the work of early Christian apologist and theologian Justin Martyr? What if it is the work of someone from one of the original congregations that the apostle had written to? Either way, it is considered the oldest copy of the New Testament, and we believe its existence adds weight to the historicity of the New Testament.

Now let's examine a cave that Church history says is the place the apostle John wrote the Revelation of Messiah Yeshua.

Cave of the Apocalypse

"I John, who also am your brother, and companion in tribulation, and in the kingdom and patience of Jesus Christ, was in the isle that is called Patmos, for the word of God, and for the testimony of Jesus Christ." (Revelation 1:9)

The Isle of Patmos, in first-century A.D. was a rock quarry island where prisoners of Rome were sent to serve their sentences. The island lies off the coasts of Greece and Turkey in the Aegean Sea. It was here that the apostle John, a Jewish fisherman by trade from northern Israel, would pen the most elaborate and significant eschatological work in the New Testament. By John's own testimony, it was here in a cave on this small island that he did his final writing around 96 A.D. This cave has been known throughout the centuries as, "The Cave of the Apocalypse."

Is this, however, the actual place John recorded the last book of the New Testament? As before, let's see if it lines up with Scripture and if it fits history.

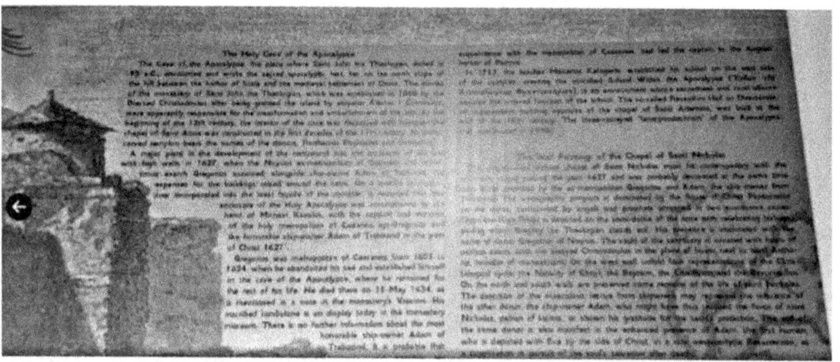

This information poster hangs at the entry of the Cave. Photographed by a visitor and posted for the public domain.

Officially, photography is forbidden inside the cave, but an anonymous visitor snapped this photo and posted it online for the public domain.

Firstly, the location of the cave. Revelation 1:9 states that John was on Patmos, which reliable history records as a Greek island where, according to most biblical historians, he was exiled as a result of anti-Christian persecution under the Roman emperor. So the location is correct.

John was sentenced and sent to the island by emperor Domitian. There is a long-standing tradition that John had a disciple at Patmos who also served as a scribe who he dictated to. The disciple's name was Prohorus, but this is tradition and is not in the account of Revelation.

Today, the cave sits in the grotto of a Greek Orthodox Christian monastery called St. John The Theologian. The monastery can be traced back to 1088 when it was founded by the Greek Orthodox church that so-named the monastery based upon the report that John had been exiled there and recorded the Revelation. The section where the cave sits is called "Chora." Both monastery and cave sections are surrounded by walls built by a man named John Christodolous, constructed during the Crusades to protect the monastery from the Seljuk Turks. Is the section where the cave is claimed to be the actual cave that the John recorded Revelation in? That's the long-standing tradition.

Or could it have been in another section on Patmos? So far, there has not been any other site on Patmos labeled a traditional site. However, that is not to say that one could be discovered down the road. Still, one thing is certain; by John's testimony, this is the island where he wrote the last book of the Bible.

Finally, let's consider the place where it is said that they crucified our Messiah.

Golgotha (Hill of the Skull)

"And he bearing his cross went forth into a place called the place of a skull, which is called in the Hebrew Golgatha." (John 19:17)

Mortally wounded from multiple beatings, humiliated, dehydrated, and sleep-deprived was the condition of the Messiah at this point of the Gospel. Nonetheless, Yeshua took the heavy cross He would be nailed to and began His ascent up the steep embankment to the top of the hill where He would die before being Resurrected.

An early 1920's photograph of the mountain. *Source: Public Domain*

Today, the "skull" overlooks a bus depot. *Source: Anonymous visitor photo posted for public domain.*

This hill is known as "Golgotha," or in English, "Hill of the Skull." This hill situated outside of Jerusalem's wall is called *Hill of the Skull* for two reasons. The first being, the face of the cliff has a natural rock formation that resembles the face of a human skull. The second is that this was the place believed to be where David buried Goliath's head after he killed him with a sling and rock (1 Samuel 17:49-54).

The picture painted of this phase of Yeshua's execution truly illustrates the amount of suffering He went through to pay the penalty for our sins. One can only imagine the view the view Messiah had as He approached the hill, looking at the skull face in the cliff with two prisoners already hanging at the top. Truly the love of God was demonstrated that day as Yeshua knew it was coming and yet volunteered Himself in order to pay the penalty of our sins. (John 12:27) Hallelujah, and glory to the Most High!

Coming soon from Betrothed Publishers

Read the whole series, available soon on Amazon.com and LittleRoniPublishers.com

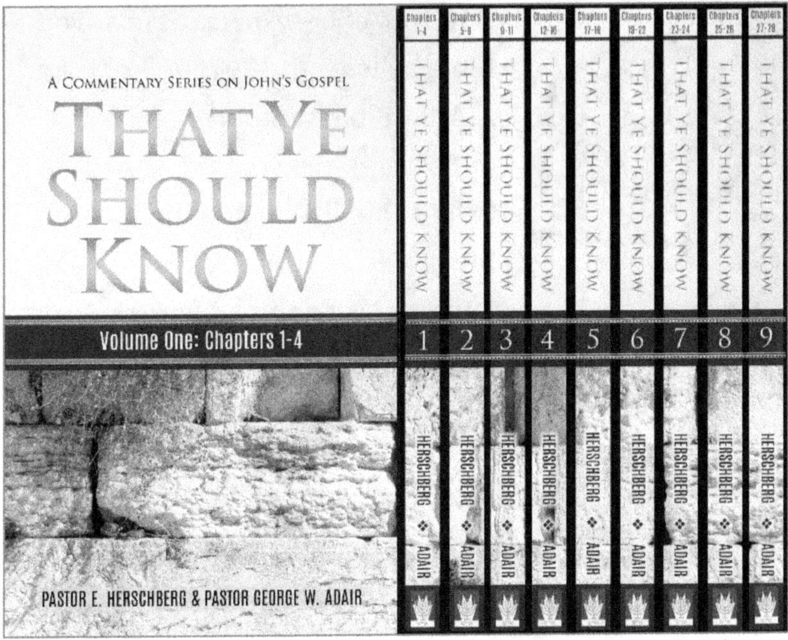

Cover simulation; actual covers still in production.

About the authors

Eric Herschberg became a saved Bible believer in 1997. He holds an A.A. in Biblical Studies and a B.A. in Pastoral ministries. Eric and his lovely wife live in Alabama where he serves as pastor of Sound the Shofar Messianic Ministries in Birmingham, AL.

George Adair is married to his wife Tricia and resides in Alabama. George received his pastoral ordination at Badlands Bible fellowship in 2015 and was licensed in 2013 at Mount Vernon Baptist Church. George was pastor of two churches, one in Alabama and one in Montana.

Books and Resources:

1) Holy Bible, The King James Study Bible. Thomas Nelson Publishers, Nashville TN. Copyright ©1988 by Liberty University, Printed in the United States of America.

2) NIV Archeology Study Bible, by Zondervan Publishing. Copyright © The Holy Bible, New International Version 1973, 1978, 1984 by International Bible Society. Published by Zondervan, Grand Rapids MI 49630, U.S.A. www.zondervan.com, Library of Congress #2005934675.

3) The Holy Bible, New King James Version, by Thomas Nelson Publishers, Nashville © Copyright 1999 by Thomas Nelson Inc. Printed in Belgium. Thomas Nelson Publishers P.O. Box 141000, Nashville TN 37214-1000.

4) The New Testament In Four Versions, KJV, RSV, PME, NEB. By Christianity Today Edition 1963. ©1963 The Iverson-Ford Associates. Printed in the

U.S.A. Library of Congress #63-23127.

5) The New Testament and Wycliffe Bible Commentary, produced for Moody Monthly, The Iverson Associates, New York 1971. Copyright ©1971 The Iverson Associates. Library of Congress #72-183345, Printed in the U.S.A.

6) The Abingdon Bible Commentary. Copyright 1929, by Abingdon Press Inc.

7) Commentary On The Whole Bible, By Rev. Robert Jamieson D.D. Rev. A.R. Fausset A.M. Rev David Brown D.D. Zondervan Publishing House, Grand Rapids MI. Printed in the United States of America.

8) The Bible Knowledge Commentary New Testament, by John F Walvoord and Roy B Zuck. Chariot Victor Publishing- A division of Cook Communications. Copyright ©1983, SP Publications, printed in the United States of America. Library of Congress #83-61459, ISBN #0-88207-812-7.

9) Survey Of The New Testament, by Paul N Benware. Moody Press Chicago. © Copyright1990

by The Moody Bible Institute Of Chicago. Printed in the United States of America.

10) New Testament Survey, by Robert G. Gromacki. Baker House Books, Grand Rapids Michigan. Copyright ©1974 by Baker Books P.O. Box 6287, Grand Rapids MI 49516-6287. Library of Congress #74-83793. ISBN #0-8010-3677-1.

11) John, by Rodney A Whitacre. Intervarsity Press, P.O. Box 1400 Downers Grove Illinois 60515 USA. Leichester England. Copyright © 1973 by International Bible Society U.S.A. ISBN #0-8308-1804-9, UK ISBN #O-8511-685-x.

12) YouTube-posted Feb 24, 2021 by Free Documentary-History. The Ultimate Relic-Quest For The True Cross.

13) Holy Bible, Giant Print, Red Letter Edition, King James Version. By Seminars Unlimited. Copyright © E.E. Gaddy and Associates, Inc. 1982. P.O. Box 66 Keene, Texas 76059, (817) 641-3643.

14) The Jewish Backgrounds of the New Testament, by Julius Scott. Baker Books, a division of Baker Book House Co, Grand Rapids, Michigan, 49516.

© 1995 by J. Julius Scott, Jr. ISBN 0-8010-2240-1. HTTP://www.bakerbooks.com.

15) An Exposition on the Whole Bible, by G. Cambell Morgan. ©MCMLIX by Fleming H Revell Co. Library of Congress catalog # 59-8719. Printed in the United States of America.

16) www.bible.org.

17) www.oneforisrael.org, The Meaning Behind The Menorah.

18) Encyclopedia Britannica

19) Holy Bible King James edition app

Non-Fiction

PASTOR E. HERSCHBERG
PASTOR CLAY ADKINS
Revelation 9,11
A Timely Commentary on CERN, Hell, & Darkness
Amazon
#1 New Release
Messianic Judaism
#CERN
#HELL
#ALIENS
Have scientists opened portals to hell?
Rabbi Eric Herschberg & Pastor Clay Adkins Discuss

DECEPTION X
UFOs and Aliens, From Genesis to Exodus
PASTOR E. HERSCHB
PASTOR CLAY ADKINS
littleronipublishers.com
ALIENs
UAPs
UFOs
amazon.com
BEST SELLING BOOK
the Time has Come to
DISCUSS THE
DECEPTION

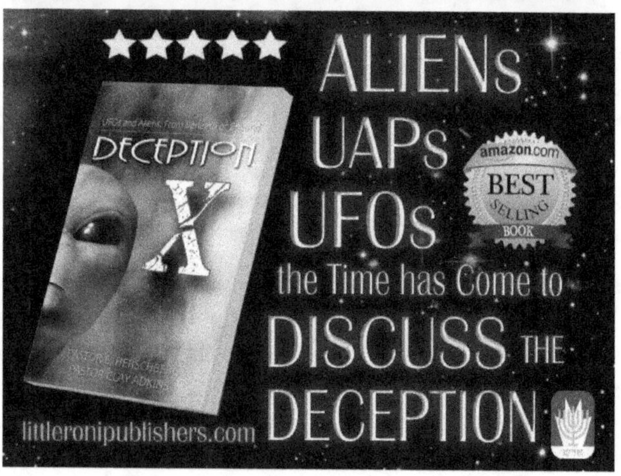

5-Star Fiction

"Thrilling End Times fiction
you won't want to put down...
I can't get it out
of my mind!"
Fascinating
NEW RELEASE
from LRP's Messianic Imprint Betrothed
ארש
LIFE BEGINS
FOURTH
AT THE END OF DAYS
RIVER
TERESA BRUCE

Christine Egbert
A Promise
Broken
A Promise Kept
A Historical Novel based on events that
led to the creation of the
State of Israel

Betrothed

Messianic Imprint of Little Roni Publishers
Clanton, Alabama
www.littleronipublishers.com

Little Roni Publishers' *Betrothed* Imprint has been created and set apart to the glory of Yeshua Ha Moschiach, our God and King.

Isaiah 58:12 | Galatians 2:20

www.ingramcontent.com/pod-product-compliance
Lightning Source LLC
Chambersburg PA
CBHW071348150726
47997CB00002B/893